Franklin Watts 1997

First American Edition 1998 by

Franklin Watts

A Division of Grolier Publishing

Sherman Turnpike

Danbury, CT 06813

EDITOR   APRIL McCROSKIE

Illustrated by David Antram, Mark Bergin, Peter Bull,

Nicholas Hewetson, John James, Mark Peppe, Gerald Wood

An SBC book, conceived, edited, and designed by The Salariya Book Co

25 Marlborough Place, Brighton, East Sussex, BN1 1UB, United Kingdom.

© THE SALARIYA BOOK COMPANY LTD MCMXCVII
Library of Congress Cataloging-in-Publication Data
Kerr, Daisy
    Bandits / written by Daisy Kerr. — 1st American ed.
          p.   cm.
    Includes index
    Summary: Surveys the history of bandits throughout the world, from the Celtic raiders to bandits of the twentieth
century.
    ISBN 0-531-14463-1
    1. Outlaws—History–Juvenile literature. 2. Brigands and robbers—History—Juvenile literature. [1. Robbers and out-
laws.]
I. Title.   97-13234
HV6441.K475 1998   CIP
364. 1—dc21   AC

Printed in Belgium

bandits

written by
DAISY KERR

Series Created & Designed by
DAVID SALARIYA

W
FRANKLIN WATTS
A Division of Grolier Publishing

NEW YORK • LONDON • HONG KONG • SYDNEY
DANBURY, CONNECTICUT

CONTENTS

Bandits are criminals who rob, injure, and kill. They have existed for thousands of years, in many countries worldwide. Usually, bandits come from the poorest groups in society and attack rich and powerful people. Often they spend their whole lives following a criminal career.

Most bandits were simply criminals breaking the law. But over the past two hundred years rebels, protesters, and terrorists have all used bandit methods to advance their political ideas.

Bandits robbed ships at sea in ancient Greek and Roman times. They seized the cargo and captured the passengers and crew to sell as slaves. The bandits also raided towns and villages along the Mediterranean coast. Greek city–states sent navies to drive away these raiders. In 67 B.C., a Roman admiral, Pompey the Great, led a fleet to fight and destroy them. He was so successful the seas around Italy stayed peaceful for the next 250 years.

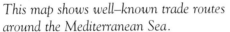

This map shows well–known trade routes around the Mediterranean Sea.

Ivory		Furs	
Copper		Wine	
Bronze		Oil	
Grain		Tin	
Gold		Incense	

Greek and Roman cargo ships sailed across the Mediterranean Sea, loaded with valuable goods from Europe, North Africa, and the Middle East. They made easy targets to attack because they followed well–known trade routes and stayed close to the shore.

Bandit boats attacked Greek merchant ships by smashing holes in their hulls with sharp underwater rams.

Celtic peoples

lived in central and western Europe from around 1100 B.C. to A.D. 100. They were famous for their skills as warriors and for their fierceness as bandits. Celtic chieftains rode off at dawn on surprise raids to attack enemy villages and farms. They drove away cattle, seized gold and silver treasures, and kidnapped women and children. After a successful raid they held a great feast.

The Celts made human sacrifices to their god Teutates. Prisoners captured on raids, and criminals, were chosen as victims. These warriors at a sacrifice were portrayed on a Celtic silver bowl made around A.D. 100.

Celtic raiders on horseback portrayed on the same silver bowl. The raiders on the right are playing war trumpets.

The Celtic warrior who showed the most courage on a raid—and seized the most loot—was rewarded with treasure and given lots to drink.

Celtic chieftains leading raids on enemy farms rode in fast war chariots pulled by strong, powerful horses.

Goths, Vandals, and Visigoths came from Germany and Scandinavia. Between A.D. 300 and A.D. 500, they set up bandit kingdoms in Hungary, North Africa, and Spain. Then Huns and Avars (warriors from northeast Asia) rode west. Under their leader, Attila (A.D. 434–453), Hun bandits demanded money from farmers, craftworkers, and merchants throughout the Roman Empire.

The splendid city of Rome was the richest and most powerful city in western Europe. It was attacked twice by hordes of barbarians. Goths attacked in A.D. 410, then Vandals attacked in A.D. 455. Weakened by these raids, Roman power finally collapsed in A.D. 476.

Viking raiders rowed their ships onto the beach, then they leaped overboard and waded ashore, armed and ready to attack.

The Vikings were sailors and raiders who lived in Scandinavia from around A.D. 800 to 1100. At home they led peaceful lives. But after A.D. 900, they began to attack neighboring peoples on the shores of the Baltic, the North Atlantic Ocean, and the North Sea. They were looking for new lands to colonize and for new places to trade.

Viking raiders attacked churches and monasteries. They hoped to seize gold crosses, silver chalices (cups), and precious books.

If members of their family had been hurt or killed by raiders, Viking warriors demanded payment or challenged the raiders to a deadly duel.

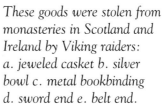

These goods were stolen from monasteries in Scotland and Ireland by Viking raiders: a. jeweled casket b. silver bowl c. metal bookbinding d. sword end e. belt end.

In Iceland, communities passed laws to stop Viking raiders attacking families and farms. They were recited every year at the "Althing" (parliament).

Everyone feared bloodthirsty Viking bandits. They called them "wolves from the sea." Warriors were ruthless and ignored enemies who begged not to be killed.

Outlaws like Robin Hood survived by catching wild animals in the woods. According to English law, all wildlife belonged to the king or his lords. Stealing it was called "poaching"—a serious crime.

A lord dishes out punishments.

Robin Hood was a hero, but in real life, outlaw bandits were wild, dangerous, and cruel. When bandits were caught, they were punished severely by the law–courts. They might even be hanged.

Robin Hood and his band of "Merry Men" are described in many medieval English ballads, but nobody knows whether they ever really existed.

Robin Hood and his band of outlaws hid in trees and then shot travelers with bows and arrows. These were favorite weapons used by ordinary people in the Middle Ages. They were cheap to make and light to carry, but they could be deadly, in the right hands. Robin Hood was famous for his skill as a bowman.

A medieval inn

Poets and singers entertained audiences in castles and inns with tales of Robin Hood's adventures as a bold outlaw, living free in the forest, and with stories of his feud with the Sheriff of Nottingham.

According to these poems, Robin was a "good" bandit who stole from the rich to give to the poor. His outlaw gang lived in Sherwood Forest, in Nottingham.

In Japan, samurai (warriors) from noble families were meant to obey "bushido"—ancient rules for honorable behavior. But low–ranking samurai often behaved like bandits as they rode around the countryside, scavenging for food and looking for members of enemy clans to fight and kill. Ordinary people, caught up in a battle between rival groups of samurai, saw their houses burned and their farms destroyed.

Samurai warriors fought with long, sharp swords and bows and arrows. They wore armor made of leather and wickerwork, which was light, flexible, and strong. Warlords sometimes provided matching suits of armor for their followers to wear.

Samurai officers rode on swift warhorses, while their low–ranking troops fought on foot. Warlords who lived by the sea often maintained fleets of bandit ships, too.

Sir Francis Drake (1540–1596) was knighted by Queen Elizabeth I of England for his pirate raids against Spanish ships.

Drake's coat of arms shows the sea and the ship Golden Hind *in which Drake sailed around the world from 1577 to 1580.*

On board the Golden Hind:
a. forecastle b. foresail c. capstan (for winding the ropes and anchor) d. boat for going ashore e. main mast f. mainsail g. rigging h. gun deck i. storeroom for cannon j. galley (kitchen).

From the 13th to the 19th centuries, many rulers gave licenses to sailors, giving them permission to "attack and annoy" enemy ships and seize their cargoes. This was a convenient way of causing trouble to a hostile government without having full–scale war. These licensed criminals were called "privateers." Sir Francis Drake made his fortune this way.

"Pieces of eight," or doubloons, were real gold and silver coins minted in Spain from metals mined in the New World. They were privateers' favorite loot.

Life for sailors on board a privateering ship was a mixture of wild excitement during raids, danger from waves and storms, and boredom during long voyages out of sight of land.

For many men in 18th–century England, becoming a highwayman was the last stage in a criminal career. As boys, they worked as pickpockets, stealing coins or watches from rich passersby.

From around 1700 in Britain and 1800 in America, stagecoaches traveled at set times along roads linking cities and towns. Highwaymen were bandits on horseback, armed with pistols. They waited by the road, ready to attack stagecoaches and rob travelers.

When the criminals had made enough money to buy a horse and some pistols, they chose a stretch of road and planned their holdups carefully.

Some highwaymen wore masks for disguise, but others were well-known and famous, like Dick Turpin and Black Jack.

Getting arrested

Highwaymen might get rich—but it was a risky way to earn a living. Often, they were arrested.

On trial

After their arrest, highwaymen were sent for trial. Judges and juries said that highway robbery was a serious offense.

Highwaymen found guilty were sent to prison. They hoped their friends would pay money to set them free.

If a highwayman was arrested and found guilty a second time, he was executed at a public hanging.

English pirate Mary Read (1690–1720) fought in the British army and navy, then joined a pirate ship in the Caribbean.

Chinese woman pirate Ching Shih controlled a fleet of 1,800 ships that preyed on other sailors in the South China Sea in the early 19th century.

Pirates were sailor–bandits, who chased and plundered other ships. They hoped to find food, slaves, and treasure. A pirate might become a millionare after one raid.

Anne Bonny (?–1720) ran away to sea with pirate Jack Rackham and fought bravely on his ship.

Pirates attacked sailors, wrecked ships, and interrupted trade. Piracy was outlawed many centuries ago.

The most famous pirates were British and French "buccaneers," who terrorized shipping in and around the Caribbean in the 16th and 17th centuries. If they were captured, they were executed.

The Cossacks were wild, warlike bandits and soldiers. In the 16th and 17th centuries, they settled in remote lands along the banks of the Don River, which flows though southern Russia and the Ukraine. The name "cossack" means "adventurer," and the Cossacks made their living by carrying out raids on travelers and traders or by serving as mercenary soldiers—fighting for anyone who would pay them. The Russian government tried to control the Cossacks, but they often rebelled against Russian rule.

Stenka Razin, chief of the Cossacks, terrorized villagers and boat people in the Volga River valley between 1667 and 1669. He led a massive peasant revolt in 1670, but he was captured and executed by the Russian army.

Thugs were well–organized gangs of murderers who lurked in the forests and mountains of India. They robbed and killed travelers as a sacrifice to Kali, the Hindu goddess of death. Thugs were often deeply religious, but they also profited from the goods they stole. Thug gangs originated around A.D. 200, and the tradition continued for over 600 years. After 1830, the Thugs were prosecuted by the British army, and Thug gangs eventually disappeared.

Tippu Sultan, king of the Indian state of Mysore from 1782 to 1799, led many bandit raids against the British, who were trying to take over his land. In his palace, Tippu kept this life-size model of a tiger eating a British soldier.

Thugs killed their victims in a special ritual way by strangling them with a scarf. Thugs spoke their own language and communicated with secret signs.

Lakshmibai, rani of Jhansi

Lakshmibai, rani (queen) of Jhansi, fought a bandit war after British troops captured her kingdom in 1857. She fought bravely and well, and people at the time said she was one of the best warriors they had ever seen. But sadly, she died from wounds in 1858.

The Mexican revolution, 1910

To many ordinary people, freedom fighters were brave heroes, struggling for independence for their country or to reform their governments. But to kings and queens, army leaders and the police, freedom fighters were criminals who caused terror and bloodshed.

In 1789, the ordinary people of France started a revolution. Everywhere, mobs behaved like bandits. They demanded a greater say in how their country was run. Over the next 150 years many other peoples rebelled against their governments. There were revolutions in South America, southern Europe, and Mexico.

The Maroons were runaway slaves who made raids on British homes in the Caribbean.

Simon Bolivar (1783–1830) led five South American countries against Spanish rule.

Bulgarian mountain bandits joined with religious campaigners to demand independence.

Klephts were Greek bandits. They fought the Turks who governed Greece.

Corsican bandits fought French and Italian rulers and in family feuds called "vendettas."

Pancho Villa (1878–1923) led the rebel army during the Mexican revolution of 1910.

In 1715 and 1745, Scottish Highland chiefs fought the kings who ruled Britain.

During the 19th century, the settlers in the western lands of America lived in danger of attack from many kinds of bandits. There were train robbers, swindlers, cattle rustlers, thieves, gunslingers, and murderers. Like the peaceful pioneers, these criminals saw the American West as a land of opportunity where they could make their fortunes. Unlike the pioneers, they refused to obey the law.

Cattle rustlers were cowboy bandits who rounded up herds of cattle roaming free on the Great Plains and drove them to market to sell.

From 1883 to 1913, Buffalo Bill, a former U.S. army scout, toured America with his Wild West Show, which included mock bandit raids on frontier towns and railway trains.

Jesse James (1847–1882) and his gang robbed many banks, stagecoaches, and trains. Jesse James was killed by a gang member eager to gain a reward.

33

Ned Kelly (1855–1880) led a gang. The members were killed in a shoot–out, but Kelly was hanged.

Why do some criminals break the law over and over again? Sometimes, they are mentally ill. Sometimes, they are dishonest. But often, they are members of a criminal gang. They are loyal to the gang because it offers them friendship or protection or because they admire its powerful ideas. But once they have joined, they have to obey the gang boss.

Al Capone (1899–1947) was America's most famous gang leader. He arranged for many of his rivals to be murdered, and he made a fortune selling illegal alcoholic drinks.

The Ku Klux Klan is an American secret society, founded around 1860. Members believe that white people are better than everyone else. They attack and murder people who do not agree with their ideas.

American robbers Bonnie Parker (1909–1934) and Clyde Barrow (1909–1934) shot and killed 12 people in four years before being ambushed and killed by the police.

Members of many secret societies wear special clothes, either as a disguise or to show that they belong. The Ku Klux Klan wear long white robes, with face masks and pointed hoods.

A Chinese Triad

Mafia members

Triads are Chinese secret societies. Triads operate in many big cities. Triad members take part in illegal gambling, drug dealing, and other serious crimes.

The Mafia is a society that originated in Italy and now operates in many lands. The Mafia have been blamed for many murders and other organized crime.

Terrorists are people who use terror and violence to protest against government policies or to try and win power for their own political group. Terrorists aim to frighten people into supporting them.

In 1914, Serbian protester Gavrilo Princip murdered Archduke Franz Ferdinand of Austria and his wife, because he did not agree with their plans for his country.

In 1984, terrorists from the IRA (Irish Republican Army), bombed a hotel where the British Prime Minister, Margaret Thatcher, and other government members were staying. The IRA bomb caused great damage and injury.

Airplane hijacking is a particularly dangerous form of terrorism. The terrorists try to take over the controls of the plane, and sometimes they smuggle bombs on board, to blow it up in midair.

Airplane hijacker

USEFUL WORDS

Althing The first parliament. It met once a year in Iceland to settle disputes and make new laws.

Ballads Long poems that tell a story.

Barbarians Rough, uncivilized people who behave badly.

Buccaneers Pirates who attacked ships in and around the Caribbean.

Bushido The Japanese warrior code of good behavior.

Chalice A wide cup for wine.

Colonize To settle in and take over an area of land. In the past, powerful nations attacked and colonized weaker ones.

Gunslingers Robbers who were always prepared to use guns.

Outlaws Criminals who have broken the law and who are on the run from justice.

Privateers Licensed bandits who attacked ships at sea on the orders of European governments.

Revolution A revolt (rebellion) by poor or powerless people against the government that rules them.

Samurai Expert warriors who took control of Japan from around A.D. 1100 to A.D. 1700

Stagecoach A horse-drawn coach that traveled along set routes, stopping at pre–arranged places called stages.

INDEX